21 SONGS
IN 6 DAYS

Learn
Ukulele
the Easy Way

Rebecca Bogart & Jenny Peters

Why You Should Read This Book

21 Songs in 6 Days: Learn Ukulele the Easy Way is designed for the person who has little or no music background and wants to have fun learning to play ukulele. Rebecca and I will give you the necessary steps to move from complete ukulele beginner to decent folk strummer in only six days of focused practice.

New! All Songs in Music Notation - and a website!

We've listened to you, our customers, and included traditional music notation for all 21 songs. The music is available both in book and at the new website.

Book + Ukulele.io = an Online Ukulele Course

Included with purchase of the book is unlimited access to the members' area at our website, ukulele.io. Here's what you'll find online:

60+ Videos

You'll get lesson videos of a pro helping a beginner, complete with onscreen lyrics and chord symbols. Unlike many other learning videos, these lessons move one step at a time and offer lots of tips on how to practice each new skill. Plus each video shows one teacher (Jenny) and one ukulele newbie (Rebecca), not one ultra pro zipping through things faster than you can follow.

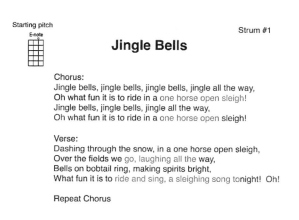

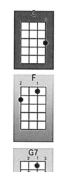

Want to check out some free sample videos? Visit **ukulele.io/free-stuff-offer/** to learn about ukulele string numbers, how to tune your ukulele, and some basics about how to strum and how to use your left hand to make chords.

All 21 Songs in Music Notation

Yes, by popular demand, all the songs and lyrics are now presented in the book in traditional sheet music format. And at the website, you can see the songs with the lyrics color-coded for each chord change.

Audio Recordings

You'll also find mp3 recordings of performances of the songs and of accompaniment tracks to play along with. There are videos to help you learn to play with the accompaniments too!

What's Special about *21 Songs*?

Our book is different from other beginning ukulele books. You'll learn one basic skill at a time and practice it in several songs before moving on to what's next. We start with the easiest possible skills and gradually build up to more complicated ones, with lots of opportunities for practice. You'll learn the 3 basic strums that are the building blocks of all ukulele-strumming patterns, and how to play the 5 easiest ukulele chords and read their chord symbols. Also, we offer lots of detailed "how to" information and troubleshooting tips, both in the book and in the lesson videos, so that if you hit a rough patch you can diagnose and solve your problems.

As one customer said, *"I have had a couple of strokes so I find it hard to retain information, but the way you are both teaching me to play the ukulele is simple and easy for me to understand. And the added bonus...it is good therapy for my hands, thank you so much for opening the wonderful sounds of the ukulele to me!"*

Learn to Sing and Strum

There are so many different ways to learn ukulele. We'll teach you to strum chords while you sing songs. Learning this way will get you off to a fast start, and you'll be able to play and sing thousands of songs without ever learning to read music. In fact, with our unique approach, you'll be able to play and sing songs after the first lesson even if you've never touched an instrument before, and you'll practice with actual songs, not boring exercises. Listed below are the songs you'll learn in our book; after mastering the songs you'll have what you need to know to learn pop songs, Christmas carols, lullabies, or even the blues.

- *Are You Sleeping?*
- *Row, Row, Row Your Boat*
- *Three Blind Mice*
- *Have You Seen the Ghost of John?*
- *Hey, Ho, Nobody Home*
- *Ah, Poor Bird*
- *Frère Jacques*
- *Chatter With the Angels*
- *A Ram Sam Sam*
- *Shoo, Fly, Don't Bother Me*
- *Hush, Little Baby*
- *Oats, Peas, Beans and Barley Grow*
- *He's Got the Whole World in His Hands*
- *Polly Wolly Doodle*
- *Jingle Bells*
- *This Land Is Your Land*
- *For He's a Jolly Good Fellow*
- *Oh, When the Saints*
- *I've Been Working on the Railroad*
- *Red River Valley*

Learn Pro Tips for Efficient Ukulele Practice

After many decades of teaching beginners, Rebecca and I know that an important part of our job is to show the student HOW to learn new musical skills. So you'll get detailed instructions on how and what to practice. We break each new skill down into small pieces that are easy to master and offer lots of troubleshooting and tips on breaking new skills down even further into mini-skills that you can learn one small step at a time.

Want great free lessons and fun tips?

Visit ukulele.io/free-stuff-offer/ and sign up to get free lesson videos and other great ukulele info, including another free ukulele eBook, *Easy Ukulele Songs: Five with Five Chords.*

Contents

Introduction

Four Sizes of Ukuleles

There are four types of ukuleles: soprano, concert, tenor and baritone. Visit ukulele.io/the-ukulele-guitar-family/ to see a video showing all four of these instruments.

Soprano, concert, and tenor ukuleles all tune to the pitches of G, C, E, A. While Rebecca prefers the tenor ukulele size and sound, I like the soprano because of its small size. It is extremely portable; I have taken it backpacking, cross-country skiing, and on bike trips to play at campfire sing-alongs! A concert ukulele is slightly larger and can be more comfortable for adult hands. A tenor ukulele has a beautiful sound because the G string can be tuned an octave lower than on the soprano ukulele. The tenor ukulele is what Izzy (Israel Kamakawiwo'ole) used on his beautiful recording of *Over the Rainbow*. If you follow all the steps outlined in this book, you will be able to play this song too. After all, several of my fifth graders were able to!

Baritone ukulele is tuned to D, G, B, E, just like the four highest strings of the guitar. Bari uke is also a beautiful instrument, and we have some of them at my school. However, since bari uke is tuned differently than the other ukuleles, I won't discuss how to play it in this book.

How to Buy a Ukulele

First, it's a good idea to try some different ukuleles before you commit to one. One way to do this is to join a ukulele club. Fleamarketmusic.com/directory offers a long list of clubs organized geographically. Another way is to shop for a ukulele at a local store, so you can try the different sizes of ukuleles to see which feels best. Ukuleles are popular right now, so they tend to sell out as quickly as they come in. Spend time trying out tenor, concert, and soprano ukuleles to see which feels most comfortable. Visit ukulele.io/how-to-buy-a-ukulele to see Rebecca and I shopping for a new ukulele at Rebecca's local music store, MusicWorks of El Cerrito (California).

Second, it is best to choose a price range and then try different ukuleles within that price range. Obviously, a $400 ukulele is likely to have a better sound that a $40 ukulele, but I have seen many instruments in the $30-$50 range that are completely acceptable. Remember that it's always easier to make a higher quality instrument sound good, so get the best ukulele you can afford.

Rebecca and I will be using three different types of ukuleles in the videos: a Fender acoustic soprano ukulele, an Epiphone acoustic-electric concert ukulele, and a Kala tenor ukulele. Here are some online sources for ukes that I can recommend.

cassandrastrings.com I've been very happy with their personalized service for ukulele purchasers.

oldtownschool.org/musicstore I have also had good luck at the Old Town School of Folk Music's store.

ecmusicworks.com We filmed Rebecca purchasing her tenor ukulele at this store. They have a large selection of ukes, plus strings, three kinds of straps, tuners, and cases. They do eBay auctions and will ship.

guitarcenter.com/ukuleles-Folk---traditional-stringed-instruments.gc?esid=ukulele Guitar Center also does a good job.

ukulelehunt.com/buy-ukulele/sellers/musicguymic/ You can buy a ukulele from Music Guy by contacting him directly.

ebay.com There is a huge range of ukuleles for sale on eBay. Follow basic precautions like checking the sellers' feedback score (make sure it is above 97 percent). Look carefully at the pictures. If they are not clear, ask for new pictures, or buy a different item. By the way, ukulele is an unusual word and hard to spell. Try visiting fatfingers.co.uk for a free search tool that will search for all misspellings of the word, ukulele. You might find a bargain!

ukulele.io/ukulele-store We've added a page to our site with links to ukuleles for sale on Amazon that we feel are good quality and value.

OTHER THINGS YOU MIGHT WANT TO BUY

To strap or not to strap

When you are first starting, you may find you can play with less tension if you use a ukulele strap, sometimes known as a ukulele thong. Rebecca loves hers and says it made playing much easier for her. The video "Tour of Your Ukulele" is located on the "Getting Started" page in the members' area of our website and shows the ukulele strap. See the *How to Sign Up for the Members' Area of ukulele.io* chapter of this book for signup instructions.

Electric tuner

While ukulele.io has a nifty uke tuner, if you want a really easy way to tune your ukulele without going online, purchase an electric tuner which fastens to the top of the uke's neck. Its LCD screen tells you whether to raise or lower the pitch of the string. If you have any hearing issues, or think it might be hard for you to compare the pitch of two sounds, an electric tuner will definitely make tuning easier and give you more time to focus on learning the mechanics of playing. Rebecca put up a short video demonstrating an electric tuner at ukulele.io/easy-uke-tuner/

You will have to experiment with which direction to turn the pegs to tighten the string, and which direction to loosen the string, because it depends on how the string was attached to the tuning peg by the person who put the string on your uke. One thing remains constant; when the string gets tighter, the pitch (sound) goes up, or higher. When the string gets looser, the pitch goes down.

What is a capo?

A capo (pronounced cape-o) is a clip fastened across the fingerboard of a stringed instrument to create a new tuning. Singers/guitarists use capos all the time to make songs fit their vocal range without having to learn new chords for the songs. The only reason you would need a capo for the material in this book is if you are learning on a baritone uke.

We used three bari ukes at our school with ukulele capos. With the capos, students could get the lovely deep sound of the baritone uke while using the chords they had learned on the smaller ukuleles. Students who knew a little guitar found the four strings of the baritone uke much easier to handle than the six strings of the guitar. We have a cool video at ukulele.io/the-ukuleleguitar-family on using a capo with a bari uke.

Set Up Your Practice Space

Human nature being what it is, you are much more likely to practice regularly if it is easy to get at your ukulele, your ebook reader and/or your device with internet access for watching the lesson videos. See if you can set aside a corner of a room, the back porch in summertime, or any other place that seems appealing as a place for your ukulele practice. Try to find a spot where other family members or pets won't be tempted to interrupt you, and you might consider turning off alerts on your phone or computer to avoid distractions. You can practice ukulele sitting down or standing up, and you will need something to rest your ebook reader on where you can see it easily while you are holding the ukulele.

A Ukulele-Sized History of the Ukulele

The ukulele is related to the guitar. The ukulele originated in the nineteenth century as a Hawaiian interpretation of the machete, a small, guitar-like instrument related to the cavaquinho, braguinha, and rajão, taken to Hawaii by Portuguese immigrants. The Hawaiian word ukulele means "jumping flea" and was used to describe the left hands of the great Hawaiian players of the ukulele. It gained great popularity elsewhere in the United States during the early twentieth century, and from there spread internationally.

Great Artists of the Ukulele

We've put some links to inspirational YouTube videos up at ukulele.io/artists. If you're the social type, like us on Facebook, as Rebecca posts cool ukulele covers on our Facebook page along with new lesson videos and other good stuff.

How To Practice - Rebecca's View

In *The First 20 Hours: How to Learn Anything Fast*, Josh Kaufman presents his ideas about how to become proficient with new skills in just 20 hours. I've organized my thoughts about practicing by using some principles about learning new skills that Josh presents in his book. You might enjoy reading the book as you start working on ukulele – but DON'T compare your progress to his. Josh was anything but a musical beginner when he started learning uke – he already had experience singing (in a choir) and with the ukulele's two-handed strum/chord coordination (he had already studied guitar).

Make time to practice

The time you spend practicing ukulele must come from somewhere else in your schedule. You will not "find" time in a big pile under a bush somewhere. We all are allotted 24 hours per day. Some you must dedicate time to work, and some time to caring for yourself or loved ones. The hours that remain are what you have left to learn the ukulele. So, you must take a hard look at your schedule and see if you can eliminate other activities that are less important to you than learning ukulele.

Another important fact about learning something new is the more time you spend working on it each day, the fewer days it will take to learn. And the faster you get good at ukulele, the more you will enjoy it. The enjoyment will make it easier to choose ukulele practice over, say, watching TV or cruising Facebook.

Make starting easy

If possible, create a space where you can keep your gear set up so that you can get started quickly when practice time rolls around. Failing that, try to store your gear to minimize setup time.

Get prepared for emotional blocks

In my almost 40 years of piano teaching, beginning adult students often have unrealistically high expectations of how fast they "should" progress. They also sabotage themselves by comparing themselves to others (sometimes real, but more often imaginary), who are, of course, doing better than they are.

Everyone has a different learning style and musical background, so things that are easy for one person may be difficult for another. As a teacher, I can definitely say I have NEVER had a student for whom everything is easy. Even the most brilliant had to work hard at something, and the ones who improve most quickly are those who are the most patient and positive, and who work the most.

Tell the negative voice in your head to be quiet so you can concentrate. It is irrelevant whether you are learning faster or slower than someone else, because learning is not a race; hopefully, it never ends, and you're not in it for the prize money anyway. Sometimes it is helpful to find someone who can support your efforts; maybe there is a friend or family member who can cheer you on. There also are a lot of great ukulele groups on Facebook and Google+ where people encourage each other and ask for help and advice.

No pain allowed

If you feel any muscular fatigue or pain while practicing, stop immediately. Fatigue, tension and pain are the body's signals that the way you are doing something involves too many muscles or too much effort. What we feel as tension is two muscles working against each other, rather like driving your car with the parking brake on. We can do tasks with tension, but it's not a good approach for the long run.

When you feel these body signals, try to adjust how you are doing the task. Look for a way to do it without tension, i.e., using only one muscle in one direction. For example, if you find holding up the ukulele and strumming at the same time fatiguing, buy a strap. If your left hand gets tired making the chords, experiment with shifting your hand and finger angles to find a position that takes less work but still gets the job done.

A final point is that when we are learning something new, we often overdo it. As you repeat each skill to make it more permanent, try to use less and less muscle effort. The reduction of effort will make playing smoother, and the reduction of tension will free brain capacity to think about other things, such as the song lyrics, or what the other hand is doing.

Work on one manageable skill at a time

Jenny and I have presented the information in small steps with lots of practice. If you can pick up the new information easily from the first presentation in the text and videos, great! But if something new doesn't improve very fast, there is a troubleshooting section that chops each skill into smaller and smaller chunks for easy digestion. Remember, everyone learns differently. One person's small chunk might be too big for you, and some of your easy bits might be impossibly large for them.

Use videos and audio files at ukulele.io for fast feedback

Once you've set up your account in the members' area of ukulele.io, you'll be able to play along with videos or mp3 sound accompaniments. (See the How to Sign Up for the Members' Area of ukulele.io chapter of this book for signup instructions.)

By listening as you play, you will get rapid feedback about timing and correct words and chords. Use the videos to diagnose whether you've got the skill up to snuff. If not, visit the troubleshooting sections and work on mastery in smaller chunks. Another plus is that playing along with the videos will help you get ready to play with other people at a ukulele club or meet-up.

Practice in short bursts

Decide how long or how many times you will repeat each step. Committing to finishing a minimum time or number of repetitions will help you move calmly through frustration to mastery.

It is easy to feel discouraged after trying something without success three or four times, but learning scientists tell us that we must hear each new fact repeated at least seven times before it is learned. And this is just to remember a fact or intellectual idea! Learning the muscular/hearing coordination required to play a musical instrument will take most people many times more than seven tries, particularly if you've never done anything like it before. So figure a minimum of 10 to 15 repetitions for several days for each difficult mini-skill.

When I am repeating small mini-skills, I find it helpful to work with a counting device. I'm not quite sure why, but using a tangible object for the count helps me feel like I am really accomplishing something, and it frees my mind to concentrate on learning rather than counting. For example, I might take 10 pencils and place them on one side of my music stand. I practice the hard section once, and then move one pencil to a new pile. Then I repeat it again and move another pencil until all the pencils have moved from one side of the stand to the other. Repeat this process for the next skill, and the next, and the next. If the skill is not significantly easier when I finish the pile of pencils, then either I repeat all 10 pencils again, or break the skill down into even smaller pieces.

In his book, *The First 20 Hours,* Josh Kaufman suggests that you "buy a decent countdown timer and set it for twenty minutes. There is only one rule: once you start the timer, you must practice until it goes off. No exceptions."

The perfect can be the enemy of the good

It's easy to get bogged down and frustrated trying to get it all right at the same time. Better to focus on improvement of one part at a time.

Let's say you were having trouble learning to strum in time to the video. You could work one to two minutes on each of the timing mini-skills in the troubleshooting section and then see if you have improved your ability to strum in time to the lesson video. If so, then go back and do each of the timing exercises again for one to two minutes, perhaps once in the morning, once at midday, and then once in the evening. Then try strumming along with the lesson video.

After several days, you should be able to master strumming in time. Then you can move on to what's next, such as Strum #2 instead of Strum #1. Meanwhile, you could work on other facets of your strum, or make chord shapes as you hum along with a video, or memorize some song words.

Finally, another good slogan to remember is "progress, not perfection."

How to Sign Up for the Members' Area of ukulele.io

Before you go any farther, please visit the link below and sign up for the members-only area of ukulele.io. The special private link below is the ONLY way to create an account in the members' area.

ukulele.io/123go

Note that you cannot create a members' area account from the home page. That's because only purchasers of *21 Songs* are eligible to access the lesson videos, lyrics and chord charts, sheet music and sound clips. You will only need to do this once. We'll send you an email with your user name and password so you won't forget them.

Once you've created your account using the private link above, then you can access the members' area from the home page of ukulele.io. Simply click the red "login" button in the upper right corner to enter the members' area. If you have any trouble creating an account, please drop us a note at ukulele.io/contact-us. We want you to start learning ukulele as quickly as possible!

Getting Started

How to Sign up for the Members' Area

Before you go any farther, please remember to visit ukulele.io/123go to sign up for the members-only area of our website. If you've already created an account, go to ukulele.io and click the red "login" button in the upper right corner to enter the members' area.

Once you're inside the members' area, scroll down and click on the link to the "Getting Started" page. This section will give you links to videos on the parts of the ukulele (including a strap), ukulele string numbers, how to tune the ukulele, left hand chord positions and thumb, and right hand strumming.

Parts of the Ukulele

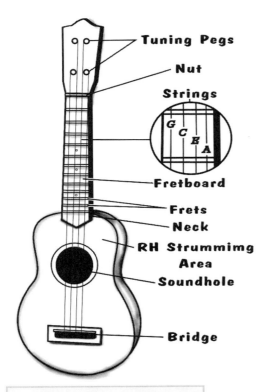

How to Hold the Ukulele

Diagram 1

Please refer to **Diagram 1** as you learn to play, so you can understand the various parts of the ukulele as I mention them in the text.

Diagram 2

Hold your uke with the fingerboard (long, skinny part) between your left thumb and index finger, and your right forearm and hand cradling the round, curvy part of the instrument. Hold the ukulele high up on your body so you can support it in the bend of your elbow, or buy a strap to hold the ukulele instead. Imagine standing with your back touching the face of a giant clock. Your head lines up with the number 12 and your feet line up with the number 6.

Point the neck of the instrument towards the number 2 to hold the uke. Holding the uke this way makes it easier to play. Check out **Diagram 2 above** for a clearer image of how this works.

The Right Hand Strums

Strum the strings using your right hand fingers. You can use your fingernails or the pads of your fingers. Some people strum using only the index finger, or only the thumb. I will be teaching you a traditional Hawaiian strumming technique I learned from my teacher, Lanialoha Lee. You should strum across the bottom of the fingerboard on the main body of the instrument, NOT where the strings cross over the sound hole in the middle of on the instrument. **Diagram 2** shows where your right hand should strum.

Just in case you were wondering, most uke players do not use a pick because it can break the ukulele's strings. We will go into the mechanics of strumming in much more detail in the section below called, "How to Strum the Ukulele".

The Left Hand Makes Chords

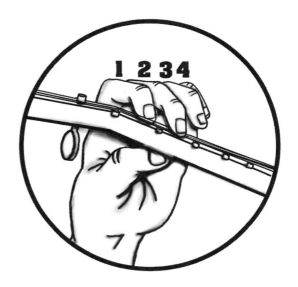

Diagram 3

Your left hand fingers should be "standing up" as you place them on the fingerboard of the ukulele as shown in **Diagram 3**. The fingerboard has strips of metal called frets. Place your fingers in between rather than on top of the frets, and press down just enough that the string is pressed against the fret. Unlike the violin, viola, cello or bass, on a ukulele the fret stops the string, rather than your finger stopping the string. We will go into a lot more detail about how to stop the strings when you learn your first left hand chord shape.

Diagram 3

Which Finger Do I Use? What Is "First Position"?

With all stringed instruments, we count the index finger as number 1. We don't count the thumb because it is holding the neck of the ukulele. So when playing ukulele or other stringed instruments like guitar or violin, you use the four fingers on your left hand. **Diagram 3** shows the finger numbers we use for stringed instruments.

Always put finger 1 (index finger) in fret 1, finger 2 (middle finger) in fret 2, finger 3 (ring finger) in fret 3, and finger 4 (pinky) in fret 4, no matter which string the fingers need to push down. This is called "first position". When you have played longer, you will learn to shift to other positions. Don't worry, that skill is in a different book, NOT this one!

The Left Thumb

Pay attention to what your left thumb is doing as you experiment with stopping the strings with your longer fingers. The thumb should be loose enough to tap against the back of the neck; you'll see exactly what I mean in the video called, "The Left Thumb", which is one of the Getting Started lesson videos.

How to Tune the Ukulele

There is a cool uke tuner and video at <u>ukulele.io/easy-uke-tuner</u>

The main thing to know about tuning your ukulele is that you need to compare the sound of the string you are tuning to a source that you know is in tune. Then you adjust your string to match the sound of the source by turning the tuning peg. Don't worry if you're not sure which way to turn the peg – there are only two directions possible, so experiment until your string sounds like the source.

Once you get your string to match the sound of the online tuner, try tuning the string's pitch higher and then lower, just to get more practice listening and turning the tuning peg at the same time. If you find you have a lot of trouble tuning with the online tuner, go ahead and buy an electric tuner as described in the Introduction section called, "Electric Tuner".

By the way, it's best to first tune your string's pitch slightly lower than the target pitch and then gradually adjust it back up until it matches. As you lower the string's pitch, you will be loosening the tension on the string. Your plucking the string as you adjust it from slightly too low to a perfect match with the pitch source will help the tension above the tuning peg nut to equal the tension on the instrument's neck. This will help keep the string in tune longer – always a good thing! Don't worry if you didn't understand this last paragraph; as you get more experience tuning your ukulele, you'll understand better how it works.

How to Strum the Ukulele

For this book, we will use three different strumming patterns. All of our strumming patterns will start with a downward movement of the right hand fingernails above the sound hole as shown in **Diagram 2.**

Do downward strums with the middle three fingers of your right hand. Adjust the angle of your strumming hand so that your fingernails rest gently on String 4, the string closest to the ceiling. Now turn your forearm as if you were rattling a doorknob and allow your fingernails to gently brush down all four strings toward the floor. You may have to experiment to refine your hand shape and the amount of pressure on the strings. Listen to be sure that you are strumming all four strings.

Before we learn about strums, let's do a 30,000-foot flyover of some key rhythm ideas.

Steady Beat and Dividing the Beat

All music needs a steady beat. By "steady beat", I mean the beats or main events in the music have equal amounts of time between them, like the ticking of a clock. You can easily walk in time to music with a steady beat because the beat of the music matches the rhythm of your movement. On the other hand (or foot), it would be difficult to run in time to a recording of wind chimes because the sounds are randomly spaced – in other words, without a steady beat.

Music would be boring if all the sounds were evenly spaced. So musicians play sounds both with the beats AND in between the beats. Often musicians refer to this as dividing the beat. Let's say the space between each beat is 1 second. Sometimes we might want to make sounds every half second, or every one-third second, or every one-quarter second.

Humans have come up with many clever and complicated ways to subdivide the beats. The important thing for YOU, the beginning ukulele strummer, to know is that there are two main ways of "dividing" the beat.

The first way is to divide it evenly. Some examples of music with even divisions of the beat are *Twinkle Twinkle Little Star*, *Spring from the Four Seasons* by Vivaldi, *Sonata in C Major (K. 545)* by Mozart, and *Für Elise* by Beethoven. In fact, most classical and a lot of rock and hip hop music use even divisions of the beat.

The second way is to divide the beat unevenly. Musicians often call this "swinging the beat". Some songs you might know that use uneven divisions of the beat are *Row Row Row Your Boat* or *The Lion Sleeps Tonight* from Disney's *The Lion King*. A lot of jazz music and early blues in particular use uneven division of the beat.

Finally, a well-known song that uses both even AND uneven divisions of the beat is the *James Bond Theme*. There's a link at ukulele.io/artists to listen to the song played on ukuleles. Try listening to all of your favorite music and decide whether the beats are straight or swung.

Meet Strums 1, 2, and 3
All of the more complicated strumming patterns are based on these three strums.

- **Strum #1** consists of downward strokes on a steady beat. It's what you feel when you march to a song.

- **Strum #2** consists of even down-up strokes played to a steady beat. It's what classical music sounds like. Listen to Mozart's Piano Sonata in C, K. 545 to get the feel for this type of rhythmic organization. You play this strum by going down-up-down-up with your fingernails brushing the strings on the down stroke and your thumbnail brushing the strings on the up stroke. This even rhythmic division is called "straight".

- **Strum #3** consists of down-up strokes to a steady beat, but the down stroke is longer than the up stroke. Think of a jazz drummer brushing the cymbal in a fancy restaurant to get the feel for this kind of music. This uneven division of the beat is called swung. *The Lion Sleeps Tonight* uses a swung rhythmic pattern.

PRACTICE TIME: Strums #1-3 on Open Strings

Watch the video "Strumming" from the "Getting Started" web page to see me teach Rebecca each of these strums on the open strings. "Open strings" means your left hand's fingers will not be pressing on any strings so you can focus on the right hand coordination and timing. Play along with the strums until they are easy for you.

Troubleshooting Strumming

Here are some steps to take if you're having trouble with strumming.

Try to isolate the problem

- Are you having trouble getting your strum to match the speed of the video/audio? Or are you having trouble making all the strings ring nicely?

- Perhaps you are having trouble on the down stroke, but not the up stroke? Or maybe you are having the opposite problem: up works well, but down doesn't. Or maybe you are having ALL of these problems at one time or another.

- Let's say you were having trouble with the timing, and with making the strings ring on the up stroke. The quickest way to solve the problem would be to focus on correcting one problem at a time. So, first practice to solve the timing problem on a down stroke (Strum #1). Then work on the timing problem for down and up strokes combined (Strums #2), and then practice making the strings ring without worrying about timing. Then try integrating the correct ringing strum with timing the down stroke (Strum #1) correctly. Finally, integrate the correct ringing strum with timing both the down and up correctly (Strums #2 and #3).

- The entire process just described might continue over two to three days, or even two to three weeks, depending on how often and how long you practice, and how easily you can tune in to the movements of your hands and arms. While you are polishing up your strumming, you can start learning different left hand chord patterns, or maybe humming or singing along with the words in the songs. You could also try memorizing the words of some of the songs.

Try doing some other, easier large-muscle activity in time with the video/audio

Large muscle movements are often easier to control than small muscle movements. So if you can't execute the strumming in time with the video, try some of the activities listed below. Once you have trained your brain to produce a muscular activity in time to something you hear, then gradually transfer the timing to the specific movement you need, i.e. moving the right forearm up and down from the elbow. For example, try:

- walking at the same speed of the strum to feel the speed needed in your legs. Once you can walk at the matching speed, then try tapping your right hand on your leg as you "walk" the strum. (This would only work with Strums #1 and #2, by the way.)
- clapping your right hand on your leg with the proper timing while standing or sitting
- strumming an imaginary ukulele with the proper timing
- strumming the real ukulele with the proper timing

Now let's troubleshoot making the strings ring

To produce a good ringing sound, you have to brush the strings with a specific amount of pressure. If it's too little pressure, there won't be any sound at all. If it's too much pressure, you will get an ugly, "twangy" sound.

Try strumming only up or down, whichever is easiest for you. Start with the lightest possible pressure, so there is no sound at all, and then gradually add more and more pressure until it feels as if you might pull the strings off the instrument. Then back off the pressure until there is no sound at all. Somewhere in this process, you probably strummed and made a nice sound. If not, repeat the process, with the goal to listen like a scientist to the relationship between pressure and sound. Don't judge, just observe. When you have a clear experience inside your body of the relationship between pressure and sound, resume the process of going from light to heavy and stop when you have a nice ringing sound.

Once you can make the strings ring in the direction that is easiest for you, see if you can transfer it to the other direction by carefully observing the amount of pressure you put on the strings. You might need to repeat the range of pressure experiment that I described above.

A final strumming issue might occur with the change of direction from the down stroke to the up stroke. Try rotating your forearm as if you were opening a doorknob. The change of direction of the forearm from down to up stroke should feel the same – use a forearm rotation to change your strum direction. Doing it this way will reduce tension and smooth out the change of direction.

Having a hard time catching the rhythm of Strum 3?

Some folks find it helpful to think of a word with three syllables and coordinate their movements to the syllables. Here are some examples:

- ❖ Pineapple: Strum down on "pine" and up on "ple"
- ❖ Strawberry: Strum down on "straw" and up on "ry"

Drop us a note at ukulele.io/contact-us if you find a word that works for you!

How to Make a C Major Chord

Now we're going to learn how to make a C Major chord with the left hand. **Diagram 4** shows where to place your finger on the string closest to the floor, the A string. As I briefly mentioned in the *Getting Started* section called, "Which Finger Do I Use?", we always use finger 1 on string 1, finger 2 on string 2 etc. Since you will be stopping fret 3, use your third finger (or ring finger) to stop the string. This will make it easier to change chords later because the other two fingers will be available to make the next chord.

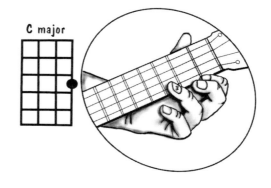

Diagram 4

Ukulele String Numbers

Ukulele strings are numbered from the floor to the ceiling when you are holding the uke in playing position. That means the string closest to your eyes is string 4 with a pitch of G. String 3 has a pitch of C. String 2 has a pitch of E, and string 1 is closest to the floor and has a pitch of A. Watch the video on ukulele string numbers from the "Getting Started " web page.

PRACTICE TIME: C Major Chord with Strums #1-3

Refer to the videos and sound clip on the "Getting Started" web page in the members-only area of our ukulele.io website. Remember, you can sign up for your members area account at ukulele.io/123go.

Be sure to practice making the C Major chord with your left hand third (ring) finger while you do Strum #1 (downward strokes on a steady beat) with your right hand. If you have any difficulty making the C Major chord with your left hand, you might want to review the video, "How to Make Chords With the Left Hand" and/or "The Left Thumb".

Now make the C Major chord with your left hand while you do Strum #2: even down-up strokes to a steady beat.

Finally, do Strum #3: uneven down-up strokes to a steady beat as you continue to make the C Major chord with your left hand. Watch the video and play along until it is easy for you. Now you're on the road! You're tuned up, and you have both hands oriented to their jobs. Time for some songs!

Troubleshooting Your First Left Hand Chord

Experiment with the placement of your finger relative to the frets. On the soprano ukulele, there may be only one location that your finger will fit. On a tenor or baritone ukulele, there are more options.

Also experiment with how much pressure you need to use. You want to use just enough pressure to make the string speak clearly. If you use too little pressure, the string will not make a sound. If you use too much pressure, the pitch will go slightly higher than it should and your chords will sound out of tune. I think you will find that you can put the string down with the least effort when your fingertip is more or less at a right angle to the fingerboard. You may have to trim your nails to be able to get an efficient angle to the fingerboard.

As you start learning chords, check that your fingertip is only stopping one string at a time. An easy way to check is to put your left hand into the chord shape you are learning and then pluck each of the four strings one at a time. They should each make a nice clear sound. No thunks allowed! (When you are more advanced, you will learn something called a bar chord, which is played with flattened finger stopping more than one string. Not to worry: this comes later!)

Your finger 3 should be shaped like a bridge when you put it on string #1 to make the C chord. Strings 2, 3, and 4 need to be able to move freely in order to make sound, just like water in a river or traffic on a road moves freely under a bridge. If you collapse your fingertips, you might get a muddy sound or not push the string down enough, which will make the chord sound wrong. In Hawaii, children are often told to make both their hands, right and left, like crabs, so they are playing the ukulele with their fingertips on each hand. Remember that ukulele means "jumping flea" in Hawaiian, and that fleas cannot jump unless they are on their tiptoes!

I didn't have much trouble learning the left hand chords for uke because I have a lot of background with other stringed instruments. However, Rebecca thought the left hand was much harder than the right, which is an example of how different things are hard for different people.

The video "How to Make Chords with the Left Hand" on the "Getting Started" page in the members' area of <u>ukulele.io</u> covers these pointers for the left hand. Remember to visit <u>ukulele.io/123go</u> and create a member account before trying to access the lesson materials - you can't sign up for the members' area from the home page.

Day 1 - Songs Using the C Major Chord

Remember to sign up for the members' area of our website at <u>ukulele.io/123go</u> *for easy access to the videos referred in this chapter. The "Day 1" page in the members' area will give you links to videos, color-coded lyrics and chord diagrams, and mp3 accompaniments for each of today's songs.*

Let's review. We have learned:
- How to hold the ukulele
- How to strum the ukulele with three different patterns
- How to make the C Major chord with your left hand

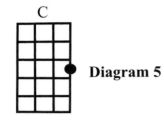

C

Diagram 5

If you haven't already, please practice strumming a C Major chord with the three different strumming patterns until you can keep the beat going along smoothly with the video. If you find this takes several days, feel free to move along into this section and work on learning words and melodies only. Now, let's make some music!

ABOUT TODAY'S SONGS

What Is a Round?

In this next section, we are going to learn three songs: *Are You Sleeping?, Three Blind Mice*, and *Row, Row, Row Your Boat*. All three of these songs are rounds, which are songs that can be sung by two groups or two people starting at different times.

For example, here's how to sing *Are You Sleeping?* as a round. First, go find another person who will sing with you. Sometimes this takes a while! One person starts singing first. The second person waits until the first person gets to "Brother John, Brother John". At the same time as the first person is singing "Brother John," the first person begins singing "Are you sleeping, are you sleeping?" So two people are singing the same song, but they are never singing the exact same part of the song at the same time. This technique doesn't work with just any song – the song needs to have been written so that it will sound good when different parts of it are overlapped. When you watch today's lesson videos you'll hear what a round sounds like because Rebecca and I sing the songs as rounds.

Parodies and Mice

Another thing you'll notice on the video for *Three Blind Mice* is that Rebecca and I sing different words about our mascot, Claire the Cat. Making up your own words to a familiar melody is called a "parody". It's a lot of fun to exercise your creativity by making up parodies to fit the situation at hand.

Three Blind Mice is a more exciting song than you might think. If you sing it at certain sports events with three referees you might get thrown out because the refs think you are singing about them. Which might, in fact, be the case, as it was in 1985 when Wilbur Snapp, the organist for the baseball Clearwater Phillies, was thrown out of the game for playing *Three Blind Mice* after what he considered a bad call. Same thing happened to announcer Derek Dye after a disputed call at first base on August 1, 2012, during a Daytona Cubs - Fort Myers Miracle minor-league baseball game.

Are You Sleeping?

Start singing on C, the same pitch as string 3.

Row, Row, Row Your Boat

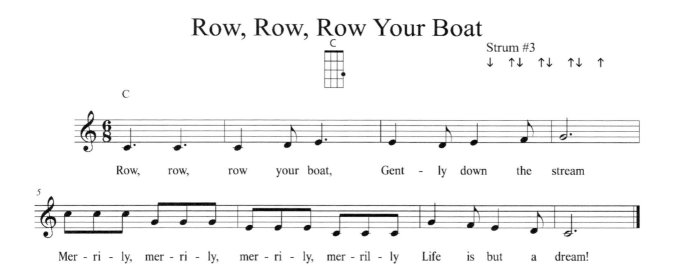

Start singing on C, the pitch of string 3.

Three Blind Mice

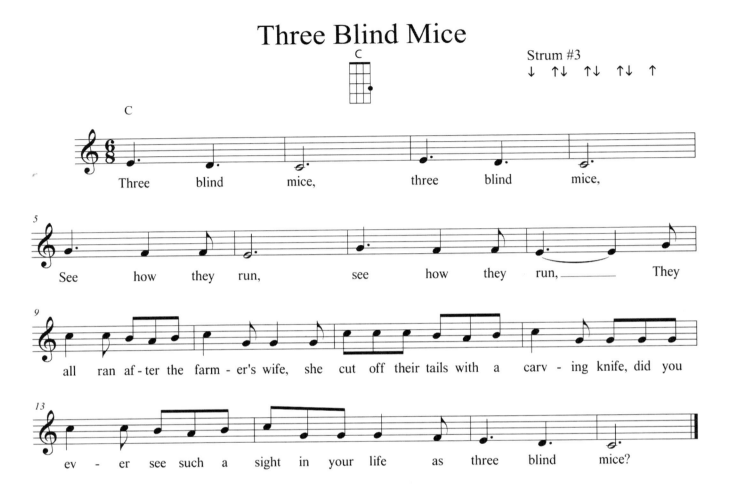

Pluck string 2, the second string up from the floor, to get your opening pitch for singing.

PRACTICE TIME: C Major Chord Songs

Refer to the video and sound clip on the "Day 1" page in the members' area of <u>ukulele.io</u>. (Visit <u>ukulele.io/123go</u> first to create your account - you can't sign up for members' area from the home page.)"

Practice all three songs until you can keep the melody and the strum going steadily throughout the song. Use either the video or the sound clip, whichever you prefer.

Troubleshooting Combining Singing and Playing

Having trouble singing the song and strumming at the same time? You're not alone. There are whole books on this subject. The first thing to do is make sure that you can do each of the skills separately. Can you strum the whole song in time with the video? Can you sing the whole song in time with the video? If not, practice each of these skills separately until they are easy.

Here are some learning suggestions:

- First, be sure you can strum in time with the videos. If not, revisit "Troubleshooting Your Strums" in *Getting Started*.
- Then learn to sing the song without playing. Listen and hum along with the video to learn the melody. Then try singing along with the video while you look at this book as necessary to read the words. If that is too hard at first, try just chanting the words in rhythm, then add singing the words to the melody you have learned.
- When you can easily sing the song, try clapping along as you sing the song, using the rhythm of the strum you will use. Doing the clapping movement with your hands will prime your brain to coordinate the strumming hand movements with singing.
- Now we're going to gradually integrate singing with playing. Try humming the tune along with the video while holding the C chord with your left hand. Next, try humming and strumming the C chord. You can always start with an easier strum, say Strum #1, and then switch to a harder strum like Strum #3 later.
- Finally, change from humming the tune to singing the words while you strum the C chord. Now you've got it!

If things still fall apart, there are several things to try.

- Go back and be sure to repeat each step until it is easy, not just barely possible.
- Next, focus in on only one line of the song at a time. For example, sing and strum the first line of *Row, Row, Row Your Boat* as many times as you need to until it feels easy, or at least improved. Then move on to the next line: "Gently down the stream." Continue until you can perform each line of the song easily.
- Then try singing and strumming the first two lines of the song in a row. You will probably have errors that did not occur when you did each of the lines alone; this is normal. Go back and review each of the lines separately a few times, and then try repeating the two lines in sequence. After

several journeys through the lines, both separately and joined in sequence, you should be able to combine the first two lines in sequence at a reasonable accuracy level.

- Next, review the third line, as its coordination has probably faded from your short-term memory. Now try performing all three lines in the correct sequence. Again, new mistakes or confusion will probably surface. Go back and review any trouble spots, and then try combining all three lines again. Repeat as needed.

If you are very new to singing or to using your hands to make music, you may find that it takes your brain a while to create the new neural pathways needed to sing and play. Spend as many days as necessary on this step, because it is crucial to playing ukulele. And remember, you're not in this to win a race. Stick with it – music is a unique part of our humanity, and connecting with your inner musician will enrich your life. There's a reason you were drawn to purchase a ukulele and this book, and only persistence will help you discover what it is.

Day 2 - Songs Using the A Minor Chord

Remember to sign up for the members-only area of our website at ukulele.io/123go. Log in to the members' area at ukulele.io by clicking the red log in button at the top right of the home page. To access the videos, color-coded lyrics, and mp3 audio accompaniments referred to in this chapter, scroll down and click the "Day 2" link.

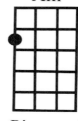

Am

Diagram 6

> **Let's review.**
>
> Yesterday we learned three C Major chord songs:
> - *Are You Sleeping?*: Use strum #1, start on C
> - *Row, Row, Row Your Boat:* Use strum #3, start on C
> - *Three Blind Mice:* Use strum #3, start on E

If you haven't done so already, please practice singing these songs while strumming the C Major chord. Like C Major, A Minor is an easy chord to play on the ukulele. Both chords only use one finger on the left hand. This is a good thing!

Put your second (middle) finger on the second fret of string 1, the G string (the string closest to the ceiling.) Remember, for this book you always use what we call "first position", which means finger 1 (pointer finger) in fret 1, finger 2 (middle finger) in fret 2, finger 3 (ring finger) in fret 3, and finger 4 (pinky) in fret 4, no matter which string the fingers need to push down.

Be sure to stand your finger up by placing your fingernail against the fingerboard at about a 90-degree angle. Be sure your middle finger does not touch the other three strings so they are free to ring.

You will notice that the A minor chord has a different sound quality than the C Major chord. Many people think minor chords sound sad or dark and major chords sound happy or bright. The two chords are structured differently in music theory land, but meanwhile, just enjoy the new sound and more somber words of the minor-key songs.

PRACTICE TIME: A Minor Chord with Strums #1-3

Refer to the videos and sound clips on the "Day 2" page in the members' area of ukulele.io.

- Practice making the A Minor chord with your left hand second (middle) finger while you do Strum #1 (downward strokes on a steady beat) with your right hand. If you have any difficulty making the A Minor chord, you might want to review the videos "How to Make Ukulele Chords with the Left Hand" and/or "Ukulele Technique: The Left Thumb", both on the "Getting Started Resources" page in the members' area of our website. Even if you already have watched these videos, new information or insights might pop out at you since you have more ukulele experience now.

- Now make the A Minor chord with your left hand while you do Strum #2: even down-up strokes to a steady beat.

- Finally, do Strum #3: uneven down-up strokes to a steady beat as you continue to make the A Minor chord with your left hand.
- Watch the video and play along with us until it is easy for you.
- Now let's learn some songs! The main purpose of these songs is to give you a fun way to practice your A Minor chord and strums. If you don't know these songs or find them difficult to learn, feel free to skip one or all of them. And just like the C Major songs, all of the A Minor songs are rounds, which means you could sing them with another person starting at a different time than you.

Have You Seen the Ghost of John?

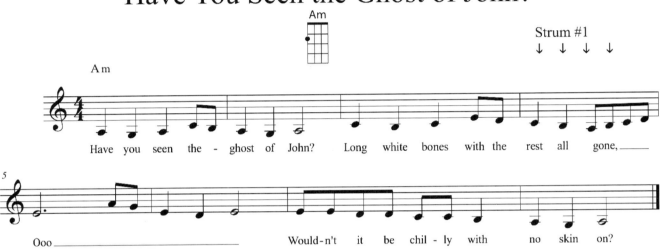

Start singing on A, the same pitch as string 1.

Hey, Ho Nobody Home

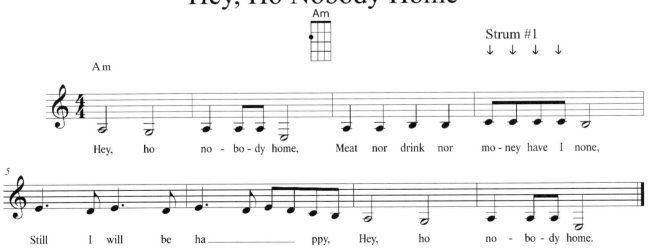

Start singing on A, the same pitch as string 1.

Ah, Poor Bird

Start singing on A, the same pitch as string 1.

PRACTICE TIME: A Minor Chord Songs

Refer to the video and sound clip on the "Day 2" page in the members' area of our website.

Practice all three new songs for today until you can keep the melody and the strum going steadily throughout the song. Use either the video or the sound clip, whichever you prefer. If the A Minor songs are less familiar, or it seems too hard to learn them all, it's fine to skip some of them if you want. The Ukulele Police will not come to your house. *Hey, Ho, Nobody Home* might be the most familiar of the three, and there is a video on the "Day 2" page in the members' area of ukulele.io showing how to play and sing this song with the accompaniment track.

Troubleshooting A Minor Chord Songs

If anything new today gives you trouble, review the same skill breakdown techniques that we used in "Getting Started" and "Day 1 – Songs Using the C Major Chord". But this time, apply the steps you need to the A Minor chord and today's songs. You may be continuing to work on skill breakdowns on the C Major songs at the same time. That's great! You're becoming efficient at your ukulele practice. Just go ahead and add some of the skill breakdown tasks to the A minor songs.

Most new skills require at least seven to ten days of repetition before they become permanent. Also, the repetition will make your playing smoother and perhaps faster as your body gets more experience playing the ukulele with two hands while you sing. So, set aside time to review the songs from Day 1 that used the

C Major chord: *Are You Sleeping?*, *Row, Row, Row Your Boat* and *Three Blind Mice.* You're on your way!

Day 3 - Songs Using the F Major Chord

For videos and audio tracks referred to in this chapter, see the "Day 3" page in the members' area of ukulele.io. Log in to the members' area by clicking the red log in button at the top right of the home page. Sign up to get access at ukulele.io/123go.

Let's review. First, review your songs from both Day 1 and Day 2, so your left hand remembers the shape and feel of the C Major and A Minor chords. Remember, you can practice the C Major songs with the videos from the "Day 1" web page and the A Minor songs with the videos from the "Day 2" web page.

Here is your current play list (the list of songs you know):

- *Are You Sleeping?:* Use Strum #1 with the C Major chord and start singing on C
- *Row, Row, Row Your Boat*: Use Strum #3 with the C Major chord, and start singing on C
- *Three Blind Mice*: Use Strum #3 with the C Major chord, and start singing on E
- *Have You Seen the Ghost of John?*: Use Strum #1 with the A Minor chord, start singing on A
- *Hey, Ho, Nobody Home*: Use Strum #2 with the A Minor chord, start singing on A
- *Ah, Poor Bird*: Use Strum #2 with the A Minor chord, start singing on A

Learning the F Major Chord:

You will use two of your left hand fingers at the same time to make our new chord for today, F Major. Remember **Diagram 2** with the big clock? The left hand in this picture is making an F Major chord.

Here are detailed directions to help you make the F Major chord. Watch the video "Learning the F Major Chord" to see these skills in action.

- First, put your first (index) finger on string 2 in the first fret. Put your thumb on the neck behind your first finger. Be sure to keep your palm at an angle to the neck so only the side of your hand is touching the neck in the area above the nut, near the tuning pegs.
- Next, put your second (middle) finger on the second fret of string 4, the G string. Experiment with the angle of your fingernail to the fingerboard to be sure you are not accidentally stopping string 3. This is the same position you used for your second finger for the A Minor chord.

The F Major chord diagram looks like this:

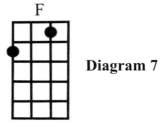

Diagram 7

PRACTICE TIME: F Major Chord with Strums #1-3

Refer to the video and sound clip on the "Day 3" page in the members' area at ukulele.io.

- Practice making the F Major chord while you do Strum #1 (downward strokes on a steady beat) with your right hand.

- Now make the F Major chord with your left hand while you do Strum #2: even down-up strokes to a steady beat.
- Finally, do Strum #3: uneven down-up strokes to a steady beat as you continue to make the F Major chord with your left hand.
- Watch the videos and play along until it is easy for you.

About Today's Songs

Frère Jacques is our first newish song for today. Actually, *Frère Jacques* is the same song as *Are You Sleeping?*, except now you will sing the words in French and play the F chord instead of the C chord. On the *Frère Jacques* video, Rebecca and I sing a second verse with words about Rebecca's cat, Claire. This is another parody like the one we created for Day 1. *Chatter With the Angels,* our second song, is an African-American work song. The singer is dreaming about a time when she/he would be with the angels, rather than working in the fields as a slave. The way it's presented in the song, I might go with the angels myself.

A Ram Sam Sam is our third F Major song. The words are nonsense syllables, sort of like the ee-i-ee-i-o in *Old MacDonald Had a Farm*. This song can be done as a round if you have someone singing with you. This song originated as a children's singing game and has fun hand movements that go with it as well.

What is a Pickup?

A Ram Sam Sam begins with a pickup, which musicians sometimes also call an upbeat. It can be confusing to know when to start singing and strumming when there is pickup, so unfortunately we will need to have a little music theory inserted here. Be patient; all this theory actually will help you play better! Jenny has made a video that explains the material below with some musical examples. To see it, click on "Day 3" in the main menu of the members area, and then click on "Song 3: A Ram Sam Sam".

A pickup or upbeat is a few words or notes at the beginning of a song that are less emphasized. For example, *Happy Birthday* begins with an upbeat. When we sing *Happy Birthday*, it sounds like:

> Happy BIRTHday to YOU
> Happy BIRTHday to YOU
> Happy BIRTHday dear so and so...
> Happy BIRTHday to YOU.

In the words, "Happy" is less emphasized (sometimes referred to as "weak") and "Birthday" is sung a little more loudly (sometimes called "strong"). "Happy" is the pickup, and "Birthday" is the first emphasized, or "strong" beat in the song. Watch Jenny demonstrate this concept in the "Day 3 Resources" videos.

Notice how when you say the words aloud in the rhythm of the song, the pattern of weak/strong beats is very regular. The musical term for this regular pattern of emphasis is "meter", "feel" or sometimes "time"; for example, "that song is in waltz time". The time of the song directly affects how you strum it, which is why all of the songs in this book are in the same time or feel.

Also, notice how the stronger beats divide the rhythm into groups. These groups are called "measures". All of the songs in this book are in the same time or feel of four beats in each measure: one strong beat, and then three weaker beats. This time is very common, and has many names: "4/4 time", "common time", and "march time" are a few. Most rock and pop songs have this feel. (*Happy Birthday* has one strong beat and then only two weaker beats, which is why it is NOT in this book)

If you know how many beats are in the measure, it's easier to start a song. Usually musicians count off a full measure and then start. But if the song starts with a weaker word or note, it doesn't start with a full measure. It starts with only a part of a measure, the infamous pickup that got this whole music theory lesson going. In general, don't strum a chord while singing the words of a pickup. Start strumming again on the first beat of the complete measure, after the pickup, to help emphasize the "strong" beat.

The first word of *A Ram Sam Sam* is on the fourth, or weak, beat of the measure (a.k.a. the "pickup"), and the first full measure of this song begins with the word "Ram". So, to to begin *A Ram Sam Sam*, do Strum #2 three times, then sing "A" without strumming. Strum an F chord as you sing "Ram" to emphasize the word.

Frere Jacques

To find the starting pitch for singing, pluck an F, created by placing finger 1 in fret 1 on string 2, the second string up from the floor.

Chatter with the Angels

To find the starting pitch for singing, pluck an F, created by placing finger 1 in fret 1 on string 2, the second string up from the floor.

A Ram Sam Sam

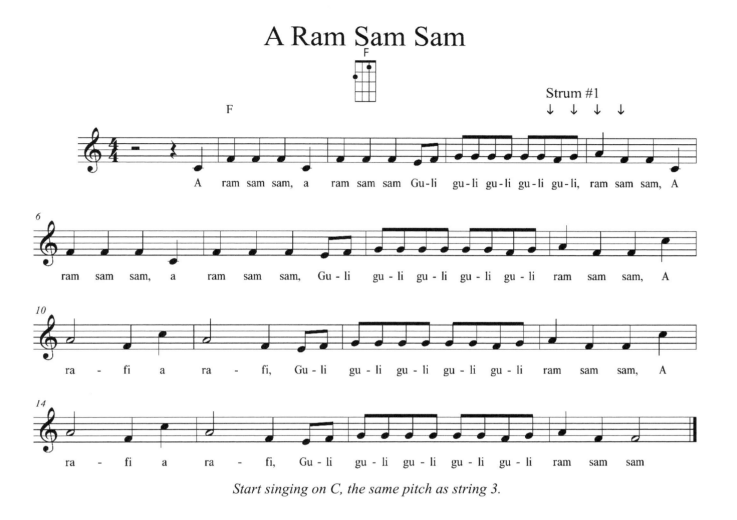

Start singing on C, the same pitch as string 3.

PRACTICE TIME: F Major Chord Songs

Refer to the videos, color-coded song lyrics, and sound clips on the "Day 3" page in the members' area of our website.

Practice all three songs until you can keep the melody and the strum going steadily throughout the song. Use either the video or the sound clip, whichever you prefer.

Troubleshooting F Major Songs

If anything new today gives you trouble, review the same skill breakdown techniques that we used in *Getting Started, Day 1 – Songs Using the C Major Chord, and Day 2 – Songs Using the A Minor Chord.* But this time, apply whichever steps you need to the F Major chord and today's songs.

If you are feeling frustrated with your progress, please reread "How to Practice" for encouragement. Perhaps your expectations are too high? Are you comparing yourself to anyone? Any comparison that is connected to a judgment ("I'm no good at this") is a recipe for feeling bad.

Try practicing each mini-skill for more repetitions or minutes. Or try to commit to more or longer practice sessions. Another trick to try is to review whatever you practiced that day for just a few minutes right before you go to sleep. Putting new information into short-term memory twice in one day can help make it permanent more quickly.

Now that you've got a few basic skills under your belt, you might consider joining a ukulele club or online group. Talking (and maybe even playing!) with fellow strummers may help you feel more encouraged about your learning process. Plus, it's fun.

Don't forget to review the songs from Day 1 and Day 2 as well! Remember it takes at least seven to ten days of repetition of a new skill before it becomes permanent.

Day 4 - Songs That Change Chords Using F Major and C7

For videos, color-coded lyrics, and audio tracks referred to in this chapter, see the "Day 4" web page in the members' area of http://ukulele.io. Remember, you must first sign up for an account at ukulele.io/123go.

Let's quickly review your songs from Days 1, 2, and 3 so your left hand remembers the shape and feel of the C Major, A Minor, and F Major chords. Below is your current play list. How many can you play without referring to the website or the words?

- *Are You Sleeping?:* Use Strum #1
- *Row, Row, Row Your Boat*: Use Strum #3
- *Three Blind Mice*: Use Strum #3
- *Have You Seen the Ghost of John?:* Use Strum #1
- *Hey, Ho, Nobody Home*: Use Strum #2
- *Ah, Poor Bird*: Use Strum #2
- *Frère Jacques*: Use F chord, Strum #1
- *Chatter With the Angels*: Use F chord, Strum #2
- *A Ram Sam Sam*: Use F chord, Strum #2

What Is a Chord Progression?

In this chapter, you will be crossing into new musical territory: songs that use two different chords. You need to learn how to change your hand position from one chord to another while singing and strumming at the same time. The "chord progression" (order of the chords in a song) using the F Major and C7 chords is one of the most common and basic for any type of music. **Diagrams 7** and **8** show the F Major and C7 chord stamps.

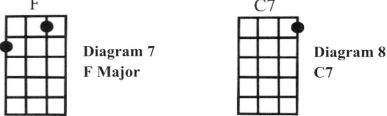

Diagram 7
F Major

Diagram 8
C7

PRACTICE TIME: Changing Between C7 and F Major

Refer to the video and sound clip on the "Day 4" page in the members' area of ukulele.io.

Because F Major uses two fingers, it can be hard to learn how to change all at once. I taught Rebecca the necessary movements in two steps. We start by moving only the first (index) finger from string 2 to string 1. Then we add the second finger on string 4 to create the F Major chord. Watch "How to Play Ukulele Chords: Moving from F to C7". It is the first video on the Day 4 page. Practice with the sound clip or the video to help you time the chord change accurately. Repeat as many times as you need until the movement is smooth and easy. Once you have mastered the left hand coordination required to change between F Major and C7, you are ready to learn today's new songs.

If you find yourself getting frustrated by the F to C7 change, which uses two fingers, try practicing the songs for today substituting the F6 chord (the chord with finger 1 in fret 1 on string 2) for the F Major chord. The F6 chord is easier than the F Major chord because it only uses one finger. Later, you can add the second finger to the F6 chord, making it an F7. (If you're not sure what I'm talking about, be sure to watch today's videos!)

About Today's Songs

Shoo, Fly Don't Bother Me was originally published just after the Civil War. It remained popular and was commonly sung by soldiers during the Spanish-American War of 1898, when flies and the yellow fever mosquito were a serious enemy. Eminem, the rap star, quotes today's second two chord song, *Hush Little Baby,* extensively in his hit, *Mockingbird.* You can watch him perform *Mockingbird* at ukulele.io/artists.

If you have trouble with Strum #3 for *Oats, Peas, Beans and Barley Grow,* you can learn it with Strum #1 first and then change to Strum #3 as you get more familiar with the song.

Start singing on A, which is the pitch of String 1.

Hush Little Baby

Start singing on C, the pitch of string 3.

Oats, Peas, Beans and Barley Grow

Start singing on A, the pitch of string 1.

PRACTICE TIME: F Major and C7 Chord Songs

Refer to the videos and sound clips for each song on the "Day 4" page in the members' area of ukulele.io

Practice all three of today's new songs until you can keep the melody and the strum going steadily throughout the song. Use either the videos or the sound clips, whichever you prefer. You could also substitute Strum #1 for Strum #3 at first.

Troubleshooting Songs That Change Chords

Today's songs are a big jump up in difficulty and also are a change to the patterns you have learned. Not only do you need to change your left hand position quickly, you have to do it at the right time in the song.

Here are some mini-skill breakdowns for changing chords.

- Practice only the left hand chord change (no strum, no singing) over and over until it is easy. This could mean five sets of ten repetitions each, which would take about two to three minutes of practice time.

- Watch the video on "How to Make Chords With the Left Hand" on the "Getting Started" page in the members' area of our website (again). Then watch yourself in a mirror, or video record yourself changing chords.

- Is your left hand position like what you see in the video? Is your left thumb loose and under the neck? Can you tap the left thumb? (This is a check to make sure it is loose.)

- Are you moving your fingers one at a time?

- If your hand position is different from the video, precisely how is it different? How can you change it to make it like the video? Make the needed change to your hand position and practice just the switch, over and over (20 to 30 times) until it becomes smoother.

And here are some mini-skill breakdowns for timing the chord change in the song.

- First, learn the song, which means learning the tune and then how the words fit into the tune.

- Next, learn which word or syllable you must change chords on.

- If necessary, use the steps in the paragraph above to speed up and smooth out left hand movements. Then try singing as you make just left hand changes. (When you place the fingers on the strings you should faintly hear the changed pitch). You can practice this way without the video at a slower speed, or one line at a time.

- Finally, integrate the strumming with the singing and left hand.

Don't forget to review the songs from Day 1, Day 2, and Day 3. Remember, it takes at least seven to ten days of repetition of a new skill before it becomes permanent. Below is your current play list. How many can you play now without referring to the videos or the words?

- *Are You Sleeping?:* Use Strum #1
- *Row, Row, Row Your Boat*: Use Strum #3
- *Three Blind Mice*: Use Strum #3
- *Have You Seen the Ghost of John?:* Use Strum #1
- *Hey, Ho, Nobody Home*: Use Strum #2
- *Ah, Poor Bird*: Use Strum #2
- *Frère Jacques*: Use F Major chord, Strum #1
- *Chatter With the Angels*: Use F Major chord, Strum #2
- *A Ram Sam Sam*: Use F Major chord, Strum #2
- *Shoo, Fly Don't Bother Me*: Use F Major and C7 chords, Strum #1
- *Hush Little Baby*: Use F Major and C7 chords, Strum #2
- *Oats, Peas, Beans and Barley Grow*: Use F Major and C7 chords, Strum #3

Day 5 - Songs that Change Chords Using C Major and G7

For videos and audio tracks referred to in this chapter, see the "Day 5" page in the members' area of ukulele.io. Log in to the members' area by clicking the red log in button at the top right of the home page. Sign up to get access at ukulele.io/123go.

A note about chord names: When a musician names a chord with only the letter, he or she is referring to the major chord. She/he will always say "minor" when a minor chord is called for. So, from now on, I will refer to C Major and F Major chords as the C and F chords. First, let's quickly review your songs from Days 1, 2, 3, and 4 so your left hand remembers the shape and feel of the C, A minor, F, and C7 chords. Below is your current play list. How many songs can you play now without referring to the videos or the words?

- *Are You Sleeping?:* Use Strum #1
- *Row, Row, Row Your Boat*: Use Strum #3
- *Three Blind Mice*: Use Strum #3
- *Have You Seen the Ghost of John?:* Use Strum #1
- *Hey, Ho, Nobody Home*: Use Strum #2
- *Ah, Poor Bird*: Use Strum #2
- *Frère Jacques*: Use F Major chord, Strum #1
- *Chatter With the Angels*: Use F Major chord, Strum #2
- *A Ram Sam Sam*: Use F Major chord, Strum #2
- *Shoo, Fly Don't Bother Me*: Use F Major and C7 chords, Strum #1
- *Hush Little Baby*: Use F Major and C7 chords, Strum #2
- *Oats, Peas, Beans and Barley Grow*: Use F Major and C7 chords, Strum #3

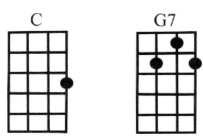

Before learning today's songs, you will need to practice changing your left hand between the positions for the C and G7 chords. You will need to use three left hand fingers at once to play the G7 chord. It will take more practice to learn this new coordination – surprise, surprise! Still, you've already logged in quite a chunk of practice time and know 12 songs, so if you apply the same practice approach, you'll be able to master this new challenge.

- Strum four down strokes while forming a C chord with your left hand.
- Now put your first finger in the first fret of string 2, and keep your third finger where it is on string 1, fret 3. This is the shape for a chord called Csus, or Csus4. ("Sus" is an abbreviation for "suspended"; sus chords are frequently used in pop and rock music. The number "4" indicates that

the fourth of the chord is suspended. The vast majority of "sus" chords are suspended 4th chords, so you can usually assume that a "sus" chord is the same thing as a "sus4" chord.)

- Finally, move finger 2 to string 3 and quickly slide finger 3 from fret 3 to fret 2 on string 1. You have arrived at the chord position for G7.
- To transition back to the C chord, lift fingers 1 and 2 and slide finger 3 from fret 2 back to fret 3.

PRACTICE TIME: Learning C to G7 in Steps

Refer to the video and sound clip on the "Day 5" page in the members' area of our website.

The first video is called "How to Play Ukulele Chords: Changing from C to G7". It shows Jenny demonstrating the *C to G7 Etude*. This is our first song using the C and G7 chords. Remember that it is easiest to put down one finger at a time instead of placing all three fingers simultaneously. The second video, "Troubleshooting the C to G7", shows some details about finger placement and timing of the finger movements. As you practice the change, the placement of each finger will become very quick so it almost seems as if you are moving all three fingers at once.

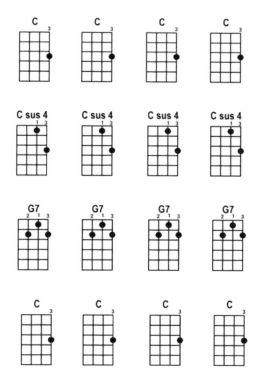

Most people find the shift to G7 challenging. If you are struggling, one way to break it down would be to practice just the first change many times (C chord to Csus chord). Then work on the second change (Csus to G7) many times. Then try doing the two steps in sequence once they are more familiar. Another way to speed up your learning is to practice just this small bit of information several times each day, and/or to review it just before going to sleep at night.

The next step is to move directly from the C chord to the G7 chord without using the Csus chord to transition. Here's a practice technique to help you start developing this skill.

- Strum C for four beats.
- Don't strum for four beats; this is called "resting for four beats". Use the four beats to move your left hand fingers one at a time into the G7 position.
- Strum G7 for four beats.
- Rest for four beats while you reshape your left hand into the C chord position.

When you can easily shift between chords with a four-beat rest, try resting for only two beats. When that is easy, try cutting the rest to only one beat. When you can handle the shift with a one-beat rest, try eliminating the rest altogether. Review this sequence until you are really comfortable finding the G7 chord one finger at a time. You can play along with the video "Practicing C to G7", which demonstrates this practice technique. Refer to **Diagrams 5** and **8** to see the C and G7 chord diagrams.

PRACTICE TIME: Intro Drill

Practice the following sequence, which I call the "Intro Drill". Rebecca found changing chords this often quite challenging. She suggested practicing it for a day before beginning the songs with three chords. We will be using this quick-changing progression in each of the songs for Day 6.

- Play C chord twice
- G7 twice
- C three times.

About Today's Songs

You're probably very clear by now on how much harder today's new chord is than yesterday's. But I have great news: all the chord changes happen at exactly the same place in today's songs, because today's songs ARE yesterday's songs. Cool, huh?

Warning: music theory ahead! New music theory concept about to be explained!

I'm sure you've noticed how you can sing the same song, even though you start singing on a higher or lower note (or "pitch") than usual. However, if you want to play along with the song, you need to match your voice to notes that will sound good with the chords that you want to play. We've learned some songs that sound good with the F and C7 chords, and now we're going to sing the same songs starting on a different pitch using the C and G7 chords. In formal music-speak this is called transposing. I've included it in this book not because I love music theory, but because transposing increases your learning speed. It's easier to learn new chords for an old song rather than new chords AND a new song.

When we transpose music, we change what is called the "key". Key is short for "key signature", which is a group of symbols at the beginning of each line of written music. The key signature matches up to a specific group of sounds that sound good together. These sounds have precise relationships with one another, and a name: "scale". There's a lot to learn about scales and key signatures, but for right now, let's just learn how to tell the name of the key you are singing and playing. (Side note: a great site for learning and practicing music theory is Ricci Adams' musictheory.net.) For almost all folk or popular music, the last chord of the song is the same as the name of the key. So for example, all of today's songs are in the key of C Major. All of yesterday's songs were in the key of F Major.

A side benefit of transposing is that it is useful if you want to raise or lower the singing range. For example, I prefer the higher singing pitch for the songs with the F and C7 chords (key of F Major), while Rebecca is more comfortable singing the lower range that goes with the C and G7 chords (key of C Major).

What Is a Verse? What Is a Chorus?

Our last two songs for today have parts called the "verse" and the "chorus". Music is often organized by repetition, but simply repeating the same music many times can become boring. To have the right mix of familiarity and variety, music can be built using alternating sections. Some of the sections are exactly the same every time and some are varied each time.

In classical music, some forms that use repetition and variety are theme and variation, rondo, and the sonata form, which is used for many symphonies, concertos, and of course, sonatas. Many popular songs are also organized using this principle.

A section of a song that has the same words and melody every time is called the "chorus". The chorus usually alternates with a section called the "verse". In the verse, the words change each time but the melody stays the same. Sometimes the verse has the same melody as the chorus; *He's Got the Whole World* has this musical design. Sometimes the verse has a different melody than the chorus, as is the case with *Polly Wolly Doodle,* today's last song.

We've printed the words for some extra verses below the sheet music along with instructions. If you are at all confused by the the written directions, remember you can watch the videos at ukulele.io to help you hear how to sing the additional verses.

To sing the extra verses go back to the beginning and play all the sheet music again singing a new verse plus a chorus ("Fare thee well...") each time you start over.

Shoo, Fly, Don't Bother Me

Hush Little Baby

Start singing on G, the pitch of string 4.

Oats, Peas, Beans and Barley Grow

Start singing on E, the pitch of string 2.

Start singing on G, the pitch of string 1.

He's Got the Whole World

He's got the little bitty baby in his hands,
He's got the little bitty baby in his hands,
He's got the little bitty baby in his hands,
He's got the whole world in his hands

He's got you and me brother, in his hands,
He's got you and me sister, in his hands,
He's got you and me brother, in his hands,
He's got the whole world in his hands.

Polly Wolly Doodle

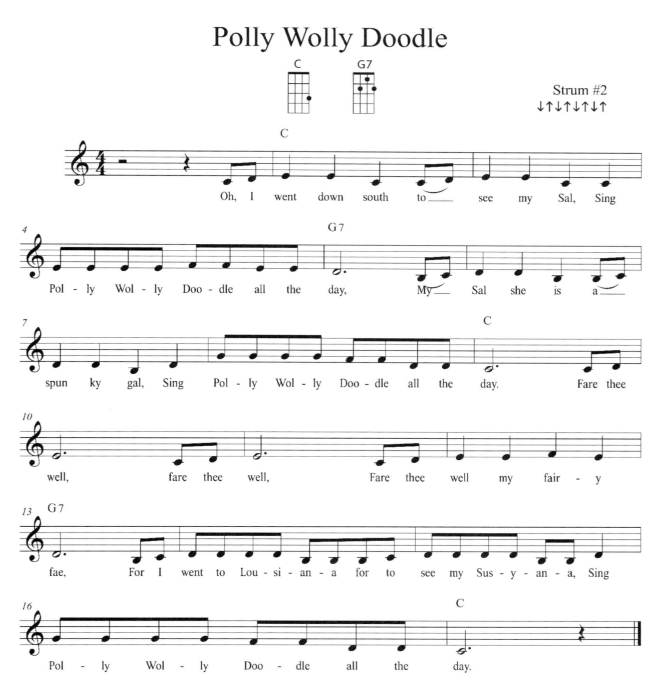

Start singing on C, the pitch of string 3.

PRACTICE TIME: C and G7 Songs

Refer to the videos and sound clips for each song on the "Day 5" page in the members' area of ukulele.io. Sign up to get access at ukulele.io/123go.

Practice all six songs until you can keep the melody and the strum going steadily throughout the song. Use either the video or the sound clip, whichever you prefer. I put six C and G7 songs in the book to give you lots of practice with the C to G7 chord progression because it is harder than the F to C7 progression. On Day 6 the difficulty notches up again, so take your time to get comfortable with the C to G7 progression! Don't forget to review the songs from Days 1 through 4 as well.

Troubleshooting C and G7 Songs: Change Chords

As always, be sure to practice only the left hand chord change (no strum, no singing) over and over until it is easy. Watch the video on "How To Make Chords with the Left Hand" (again) on the "Getting Started" page in the members' area of our website. Watch yourself in a mirror or make a video of yourself.

- Is your left hand position like what you see on the website video?
- Is the left thumb loose and under the neck?
- Are you moving the fingers one at a time?
- Is your palm at a 45-degree angle to the neck of the uke? Let your first finger rest against the uke above the nut. (Refer back to **Diagram 1** to double check where the nut is.)
- If it is different, how is it different? Make the needed change to your hand position and practice just the switch, over and over (20 to 30 times) until it becomes smoother.

Congratulations on learning songs with C and G7 chords! You've passed a major milestone in your learning journey, because G7 is the hardest chord in this book.

Day 6 - Songs that use C, F and G7

For videos, color-coded lyrics and audio tracks referred to in this chapter, see the "Day 6" page in the members' area of ukulele.io. Sign up to get access at ukulele.io/123go.

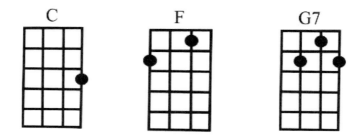

Today we will be learning songs that use three chords: C Major, F Major and G7. After all your hard work on learning the G7, you can now enjoy the richer sound of songs with three different chord sounds. Knowing these three chords will make it possible for you to play hundreds of other songs, because these chords make up one of the most common chord progressions used in all Western music. Cool, eh?

About Today's Songs

An Italian Music Term Intrudes into a Happy Holiday Tune

Did you notice that the sheet music for *Jingle Bells* says "Fine"? That's Latin for "finish", and it means you'll be ending the song there when you finish singing all the verses. "DC al Fine" stands for "Da Capo al Fine". "Capo" means "head" in Italian, and "Da Capo al Fine" means to go back to the beginning of the song and play until you see the word "Fine". Fun music fact: jazz players often refer to the chorus of the song as the "head".

For *Jingle Bells*, the music from the beginning until the word "Fine" is the chorus, and the music after "Fine" until "DC al Fine" is the verse. To sing the second verse, you would ignore the instruction to "finish" and sing the tune that goes with "Dashing through the snow..." but substitute the words for Verse 2. When you reach the end of the sheet music it's time to start following directions again. Go back to the beginning, or head, and sing the chorus one last time before you finish at the "Fine".

Some Strumming Tips

This Land Is Your Land is our second song with three chords. Use Strum #1 at first, so you can concentrate on the changes in the left hand. As you get more comfortable with this song, you can change to Strum #2. Watch "Learning *This Land is Your Land*" on the "Day 6" page in the members' area of our website to see a way to alter Strum #1 to give yourself more time to change chords. (Due to technical difficulties, the video does not show all the verses. This might be a good thing for some of you!) Start singing on C, the pitch of string 3.

For the song, *For He's a Jolly Good Fellow,* use Strum #1 because there are a lot of fast chord changes in this song. To learn the fancy strumming pattern I use when the music pauses at the end of the second line of the song, watch the video called "Learning *For He's a Jolly Good Fellow*" on the "Day 6" page in the members' area of ukulele.io.

Be sure to watch "Learning *Oh, When the Saints*" video on the "Day 6" page in the members' area of our website so you can see where we stop the strumming pattern to add drama.

Pickup Reminder
A final note: many of today's songs begin with a pickup or upbeat, which is an incomplete measure that occurs before the first complete measure of a song. We first learned about pickups, or upbeats, in Day 3 with *A Ram Sam Sam*. To briefly review, don't strum a chord during the upbeat. Instead, wait to start strumming until the first full measure. *This Land is Your Land, For He's a Jolly Good Fellow, Oh When the Saints* and *Red River Valley* all have pickups. There are directions on how to play an introduction for each song and how to transition between the introduction to the pickup and then on into the song. You'll probably find it easiest to learn the songs by watching the videos at least once or twice to hear how the strumming patterns and introductions sound. It's often easiest to learn a song without an introduction first, and then add the introduction after you've mastered the song.

Verse & Chorus
Today's songs have three different organizations.

- No verse or chorus: *I've Been Working on the Railroad, For He's a Jolly Good Fellow.* Sing these songs straight through then stop. Easy, Easy, Easy!
- Alternating verse and chorus: *Jingle Bells* and *Red River Valley* are usually sung alternating between verse and chorus, i.e. Chorus - Verse - Chorus - Verse - Chorus. For *Jingle Bells*, the verse has a different melody than the chorus. For *Red River Valley* the music is the same for the verse and the chorus.
- Just lots of verses in a row: Because there aren't choruses for *This Land is Your Land*, or *Oh When the Saints*, they are usually sung one verse after the other, like this: Verse 1 - Verse 2 - Verse 3.

Jingle Bells

Start singing on E, the pitch of string 2

This Land is Your Land

Verses:
As I was walking that ribbon of highway
I saw above me an endless skyway
I saw below me a golden valley
This land was made for you and me.

I've roamed and rambled and I've followed my footsteps
To the sparkling sands of her diamond deserts
And all around me a voice was sounding
This land was made for you and me.

The sun came shining as I was strolling
The wheat fields waving and the dust clouds rolling
The fog was lifting, a voice came chanting
This land was made for you and me.

Start singing on C, the pitch of string 3.

For He's a Jolly Good Fellow

Start singing on G, the pitch of string 4.

Oh When the Saints

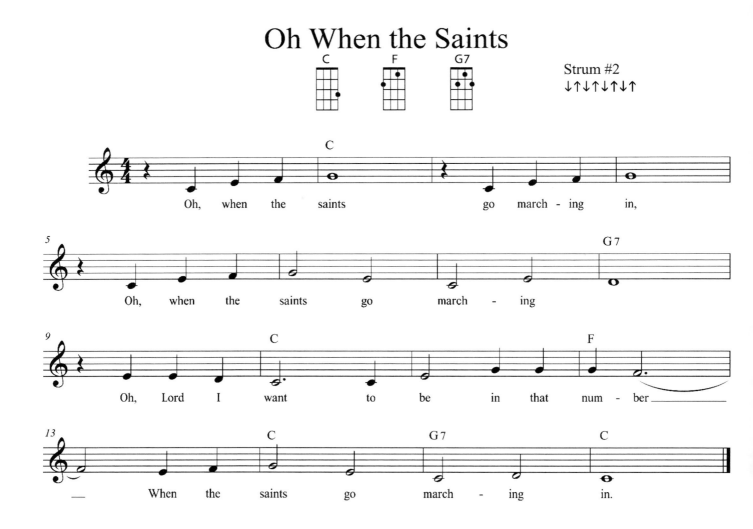

Oh, when the drums begin to bang
Oh, when the drums begin to bang
Oh, Lord I want to be in that number
When the saints go marching in.

Start singing on C, the pitch of string 3.

I've Been Working on the Railroad

Start singing on C, the pitch of string 3.

Red River Valley

Verses:
Come and sit by my side, if you love me
Do not hasten to bid me adieu
Just remember the Red River Valley
And the cowboy who loved you so true.

I've been thinking a long time, my darling
Of the sweet words you never would say
Now, alas, must my fond hopes all vanish
For they say you are going away.

Do you think of the valley you're leaving
O how lonely and how dreary it will be
And do you think of the kind hearts you're breaking
And the pain you are causing to me?

Start singing on G, the pitch of string 4.

PRACTICE TIME: C, F and G7 Songs

Refer to the video and sound clips on the "Day 6" page in the members' area of <u>ukulele.io</u>. Be sure to sign up for your account first at <u>ukulele.io/123go</u>.

Practice all six songs until you can keep the melody and the strum going steadily throughout the song. Use either the video or the sound clip, whichever you prefer.

Troubleshooting Songs with Three Chords

Today's songs are a big jump up in musical complexity because they have three chords instead of two. As always, be sure to practice only the left hand chord changes (no strum, no singing) over and over until it is easy. Remember, it's easier to be sure you repeat enough if you use a timer or counter. Watch the video on "How To Make Chords with the Left Hand" (again) from the "Getting Started" page in the members' area of our website. Watch yourself in a mirror or on a video.

- Is your left hand position like what you see on the website video?
- Is your left thumb loose and under the neck?
- Are you moving your fingers one at a time?
- Is your palm at a 45-degree angle to the neck of the uke? Let your first finger rest against the uke above the nut. (Refer back to **Diagram 1** to double check where the nut is.)
- If it is different, how is it different? Make the needed change to your hand position and practice just the switch, over and over (20 to 30 times) until it becomes smoother.

Especially now that there are three chords, you might want to apply this micro-skill breakdown to just the changes or timing that are hard for you. You may also have to focus on learning the song separately from the changes, and then learn how the changes relate to the song. Don't forget to review some of the songs from Days 1 through 5 as well. Choose your favorites, or the ones that still present challenges. Isn't it great to know so many songs that you can't easily practice them all in one sitting? Congratulations!

Day 7 - Enjoying What You Know

In this book, you have learned 21 songs in 6 days. CONGRATULATIONS! Today would be a good day to solidify what you know by playing all your songs:

Complete Play List

- *Are You Sleeping?:* Use Strum #1
- *Row, Row, Row Your Boat*: Use Strum #3
- *Three Blind Mice*: Use Strum #3
- *Have You Seen the Ghost of John?:* Use Strum #1
- *Hey, Ho, Nobody Home*: Use Strum #2
- *Ah, Poor Bird*: Use Strum #2
- *Frère Jacques*: Use F chord, Strum #1
- *Chatter With the Angels*: Use F chord, Strum #2
- *A Ram Sam Sam*: Use F chord, Strum #2
- *Shoo, Fly Don't Bother Me*: Use F and C7, Strum #1
- *Hush Little Baby*: Use F and C7, Strum #2
- *Oats, Peas, Beans and Barley Grow*: Use F and C7, Strum #3
- *C, then G7 Etude*: Boring but very useful
- *Shoo Fly Don't Bother Me*: Use C and G7, Strum #1, start singing on E
- *Hush Little Baby*: Use C and G7 chords, Strum #2, start singing on G
- *Oat, Peas, Beans and Barley Grow*: Use C and G7 chords, Strum #3, start singing on E
- *He's Got the Whole World*: Use C and G7 chords, Strum #1, start singing on G
- *Polly Wolly Doodle*: Use C and G7 chords, Strum #2, start singing on C
- *Jingle Bells*: Use C, G7 and F, Strum #1, start singing on E
- *This Land is Your Land*: Use C, G7 and F, Strum #1 or #2, start singing on C
- *For He's a Jolly Good Fellow*: Use C, G7 and F, Strum #1 or #2, start singing on G
- *Oh, When the Saints*: Use C, G7 and F, Strum #1, start singing on C
- *I've Been Working on the Railroad*: Use C, G7 and F, Strum #1 or #2, start singing on C
- *Red River Valley*: Use C, G7 and F, Strum #2, start singing on G

If you like singing and strumming the ukulele, keep a lookout for the email announcing when our next ukulele book is released. In *21 More Easy Ukulele Songs,* as we're calling it right now, we'll introduce more complicated strumming patterns to give you a more polished sound, and add A Minor and C7 chords to our three-chord songs to make new five-chord versions. We'll also show you how to read traditional "lead sheet" notation with chord stamps or chord symbols, so you can understand how to choose your own music from the many resources available on the web. And you'll learn to read tab, which is a cool shorthand notation that helps you play melodies on your ukulele. Finally, we'll learn both some traditional Hawaiian songs and the 12 bar blues. We hope you will be excited about what you have learned so far and will want to purchase *21 More Easy Ukulele Songs* when it becomes available.

An example of a song with 5 chords is the following version of *This Land Is Your Land*. If this seems complicated, that's because it is! Learn the simpler version of *This Land Is Your Land* from Day 6 before you start the more complicated version. Both versions work for the song, but the more complicated one sounds smoother and more polished. Enjoy!

INTRO: Play C chord twice, then G7 twice, then C three times. Sing, "This land is" without strumming. Start strumming the F chord on "your land".

This Land Is Your Land

Verses:
As I was walking that ribbon of highway
I saw above me an endless skyway
I saw below me a golden valley
This land was made for you and me.

I've roamed and rambled and I've followed my footsteps
To the sparkling sands of her diamond deserts
And all around me a voice was sounding
This land was made for you and me.

The sun came shining as I was strolling
The wheat fields waving and the dust clouds rolling
The fog was lifting, a voice came chanting
This land was made for you and me.

Start singing on C, the pitch of string 3

We hope you have enjoyed getting started on the ukulele. We'd love to see you on our Facebook page, on YouTube or hear from you at ukulele.io/contact-us. You can find our complete contact information in the "About the Authors" section.

Happy Strumming!

Rebecca and Jenny

Glossary

Accidental -a *flat, sharp,* or *natural*.

Bar - same as a *measure*. A measure is the space on a musical staff between two bar lines. Every measure begins with a strong beat.

Bar lines - the vertical lines on the musical and tab staffs that go from the top line of the staff to the bottom line of the staff. Bar lines are longer than note stems and do not touch any notes.

Beat - regularly timed sounds that occur the same distance apart in time in a row. Examples of sounds with a beat are the sound your heart makes, i.e. a heartbeat, or the sound of someone dribbling a basketball.

Blue notes - a note or group of notes that are different than the notes used in Western folk music. Usually in the the blues we play the different note near its next-door note so our ears can imagine the note that belongs in the African scale. In staff notation, a blue note will have a flat, sharp or natural in front of it.

Blues scale - a group of musical sounds that are spaced in the specific way that is used in blues music. The blues scale probably came with African people to the United States. For the blues songs in this book we are playing in the key of C, which is the same as all the white keys on the piano. When we add a black key to the white key scale, the music sounds different. The black key, for example, E flat, added in on top of the white key, for example, E, give the music a bluesy feel. The added black key notes are an attempt to approximate African scales. Western folk music tends to use 8 notes per octave, while African folk music tends to use 5 notes equally spaced per octave. Some of these African scale notes do not exist in Western musical instruments. For example, if you look at a piano keyboard, you can see that there ARE five black keys but the spaces between them are not equal. Thus, when you sing or play a flat note and somebody else is playing a regular note, your ear hears the sound the flat note and the regular note make together as bluesy.

Braguinha - a Portuguese fretted string instrument, like a small guitar, that was an ancestor of the ukulele.

Cavaquinho - another Portuguese fretted string instrument like the braguinha.

Chord - two or more sounds played at the same time. On the ukulele, chords usually are four sounds together because the ukulele has four strings.

Chord progression - order of chords in a song

Chord stamp - a symbol or drawing of the ukulele strings with little dots that represent where to place your fingers on the fretboard to make the chord.

GLOSSARY

Etude - a piece of music that is designed to help you learn and practice a new musical skill. Etude means study in French so etudes are sometimes called studies.

Finger numbers - these are applied to the left hand. Finger 1 is the index or "pointer" finger; finger 2 is the middle finger; finger 3 is the ring finger; and finger 4 is the pinky. For playing ukulele, we do not count the thumb because it is behind the neck of the ukulele and not available to stop a string (see "stopping").

First Position - means your finger 1 (index finger) is in the first fret, the one closest to the tuning pins.

Flat - a musical symbol placed in front of musical note. It means to lower the sound slightly, by the amount that musicians call a "half step". When you look at a blues scale, you can see a little sign that looks like a small letter "b" next to some of the notes. That sign is called is a flat and it lowers the pitch of the note by 1/2 step.

Fretboard - the long skinny part of the ukulele with metal strips in it. It is usually made of a different color wood than the larger curvy part of the instrument.

Fretting - pushing the strings against the fretboard with the fingers of your left hand so each note you play sounds clear. "Fretting" means the same thing as "stopping".

Frets - strips of metal that run across the short dimension of the long skinny fretboard. When you push down a string with your finger in between the frets, the string is held very tightly against the fret.

Guitar - a large fretted string instrument. It usually has six or more strings in comparison to the ukulele's four strings.

Key - short for "key signature", which is a group of flats or sharps at the beginning of each line of written music. The key signature matches up to a specific group of sounds that sound good together. These sounds have precise relationships with one another, and a name: "scale". Usually the name of the key is the same as the name of the chord that starts or ends the song. For most folk and pop music the starting and ending chords are the same.

Lead sheet - a way of writing out a song without using notes on a musical staff to show the pitches of the melody. Instead, the words are written out with chord stamps above them. You have to learn the melody of the song from hearing it sung to be able to use a lead sheet of a song.

Machete - another small guitar-like instrument like the braguinha, cavaquinho, and rajao.

Major - a type of chord. The distances between the pitches of a major chord make it sound happy or bright to most people.

Measure - The space on a musical staff between two bar lines. Every measure begins with a strong beat.

Melody - notes played one at time, one after the other.

Minor - another type of chord. The pitch relationships of a minor chord make it sound dark or sad to most people.

Musical improvisation - to make up music as you are playing.

Natural - a musical symbol placed in front of a musical note. It cancels any sharp or flat symbol that would normally apply to that note.

Note - a round symbol that is placed on a line or space of a musical staff. Some notes are circles or ovals; other types of notes are circles or ovals with lines attached. Each note represents one sound. The color of the note head (round part) combined with the stem (the vertical line) indicates how long each sound should last. Sometimes the word "note" is used to refer to just the sounds. For example, you might say "she played a lot of notes in that song".

Nut - the raised ridge at the top of the ukulele fretboard. It holds the strings away from the fretboard slightly so they can vibrate.

Octave - distance to the same letter note, either higher or lower. You might hear an octave in action when your mom and dad sing the same note and your dad's voice is lower and your mom's is higher, but they both sound like they are singing the same note. In Western folk music we have eight notes in an octave. "Oct" means "eight". Two other examples of words that use "oct" to mean eight are octagon and octopus.

Pickup - Almost all music is organized into patterns of strong and weak beats. One very common pattern is strong-weak-weak-weak. Almost all the songs in this book use this pattern. Another common pattern is strong-weak-weak. *Amazing Grace* uses this pattern. A pickup means the music begins on a weak beat instead of a strong beat.

Pitch - whether a sound is high or low. An example of a high sound would be birds tweeting. An example of a low sound would be a thunderstorm.

Pluck - pulling your finger against a string firmly and then gradually releasing it so the string vibrates and you hear a nice clear musical sound.

Rajão - a Portuguese fretted string instrument, similar to a small guitar. Braguinha, cavaquinho and machete are other similar instruments.

Rhythm - how sounds make patterns in time. For example, a rainstorm has a different rhythm than a rooster crowing.

Round - a song that can be sung by two groups or two people starting at different times. This way of singing doesn't work with just any song – the song needs to have been written so that it will sound good when different parts of it are overlapped.

Scale - a ladder of musical notes arranged in a specific pattern, usually with small distances in pitch all going up or down. The names of some common types of scales in Western music are major, minor, and blues. There are hundreds of types of scales in the world.

Second position - means your finger 1 (index finger) is in the second fret, one fret away from the tuning pins.

Sharp - a musical symbol placed in front of musical note. It means to raise the sound slightly, by the amount which musicians call a "half step".

Stopping- pushing a string against the fretboard with a finger of your left hand so that one end of the string rests against a fret. The other end of the string is tied to the bridge. We say the fret is "stopping" the string because the string can't vibrate where it is being pushed onto the fret. The contact with the fret shortens the amount of the string that is vibrating. Only the part of the string that is in the air and not touching anything is free to vibrate.

Sound hole - round hole in the body of the ukulele.

Staff - a musical staff is made of five equally spaced horizontal lines. There are four spaces. Each line and space of the musical staff represents a specific musical pitch. A tab staff is also made of equally spaced horizontal lines, but there are four instead of five. See "tab staff".

Stem - a vertical line attached to the round part of a musical note. The stem helps indicate the rhythm of the note. Note stems are shorter than bar lines and are attached directly to a round note symbol.

String numbers - ukulele strings are numbered from the floor to the ceiling when you are holding the uke in playing position. That means the string closest to your eyes is string 4 with a pitch of G. String 3 has a pitch of C. String 2 has a pitch of E, and string 1 is closest to the floor and has a pitch of A.

Strum 1- downward strums with a steady beat. Another way to think of it is down strums with equal time between each strum so that the strums sound evenly spaced in time.

Strum 2 - even down-up strokes played with a steady beat. This means there is an equal amount of time between each down and up strum so they sound evenly spaced in time.

Strum 3 - down-up strokes to a steady beat, but the time after the down stroke is longer than the time after the up stroke. Some of the songs in this book such as *Row, Row, Row Your Boat* and *Oats, Peas, Beans, and Barley Grow* use a 6/8 time signature. The pattern of beats in 6/8 time is STRONG-weak-weak STRONG-weak-weak. Usually when we strum a song with a 6/8 time signature we use Strum 3. We do a down strum on the STRONG and an up strum on the second weak beat just before the next STRONG. Most listeners will hear this music as having steady beats that are unevenly divided. Your feeling when you play will be long-short long-short. This long-short pattern is the feeling of Strum 3.

Tablature, or tab staff - a staff especially for fretted stringed instruments including the ukulele. Each line represents one string of the ukulele. There are numbers on the tab staff that tell the player which fret to stop the string on.

Third position - means your finger 1 (index finger) is in the third fret, two frets away from the tuning pins.

Time signature - the numbers at the beginning of each song on the staff immediately to the right of the clef. It tells you how many beats are in each measure and what the pattern of strong and weak beats is in the song. The 4/4 time signature has the pattern strong-weak-weak-weak. The 3/4 time signature has the pattern strong-weak-weak. The 6/8 time signature has the pattern STRONG-weak-weak STRONG-weak-weak. Every measure begins with a strong beat.

Tuning pegs - located just beyond the nut. Each string is wound around a tuning peg. You can change the pitch of the string by turning the peg to tighten or loosen the string. Tightening the string makes the pitch go higher (a sound more like birds chirping or a girl's voice). Loosening the string makes the pitch go down (a sound more like thunderstorm or a man's voice).

Transposing - playing or singing music starting on a different pitch but keeping the same sound to the melody and chords. When we transpose music, we change what is called the "key".

Work song - a song people sing while working to help them stay together or to express their feelings about their job.

One Last Thing...

You can help other folks trying to decide which ukulele lesson book to buy by sharing your opinions of *21 Songs in 6 Days* at Amazon.com – You can review it at: goo.gl/QbUPJK.

Thank you in advance!

About the Authors

Jenny Peters is one part of the sister duo responsible for *21 Songs in 6 Days*. She stumbled upon the ukulele after finding 45 of them in one of her elementary school classrooms. Convinced she could turn her find into more than a whole lot of noise, she designed a program to teach all of her students to play successfully with only 30 minutes of class time a week. No one was more grateful than the teacher in the next classroom.

A former private piano teacher in Chicago with a Masters in Piano Performance from the University of Illinois, Jenny now lives in Highland Park, Illinois. Married with three kids, she shares her home with three cats and more musical instruments than she would care to name.

Rebecca Bogart is the second half of the sister writing team. An acclaimed classical pianist, performer and teacher, Rebecca has been passionate about the piano and music her entire life. She has played for audiences in Italy, taught master classes at Harvard and won more than a few piano competitions. She made her solo debut at Carnegie Hall in early 2014.

Jenny Peters jenny@ukulele.io

Rebecca Bogart rebecca@ukulele.io

facebook.com/21Songsin6Days

Google+ google.com/+Ukuleleio

YouTube ukulele.io/visitYoutube

Recommended Reading

Here are some other great ukulele resources to check out:

21 Songs in 6 Days Classroom Edition: Teacher Manual and ***21 Songs in 6 Days Classroom Edition: Student*** Book by Rebecca Bogart and Jenny Peters: includes a teacher manual, student book and complete audio/video teaching curriculum. Designed so you can successfully teach kids (grades 4-8) how to play the ukulele in as little as 30 minutes a week. Includes melody tabs and dedicated chapter on blues improvisation.

21 Easy Ukulele Songs for Christmas by Rebecca Bogart and Jenny Peters: 21 seasonal favorites arranged in order of difficulty. Each song is presented with tab melodies, and a variety of strumming patterns are suggested.

Easy Ukulele Songs: Five with Five Chords by Rebecca Bogart and Jenny Peters: Continue playing five chord songs and tab melodies year round with this short book. Comes with 10 lesson videos to help you learn the songs.

Ukulele Mastery Simplified by Erich Andreas: Now that you've finished our book, you should be able to tackle the three-chord songs that begin this book.

Ukulele For Dummies by Alistair Wood: Another good book to try next. Also begins with three-chord songs.

The Daily Ukulele by Jim Beloff: This fabulous book is full of good songs – most of the recent tunes are from the 60s and 70s. There is no lesson information, but now that you know five chords you should be able to tackle some of them.

The Daily Ukulele Leap Year Edition by Jim Beloff: More fabulous songs from Jim. This version has more modern tunes by groups such as Black Keys and Green Day.

Easy Songs for Ukulele by Lil' Rev: Fingerpick the melodies of 20 pop, folk, country, and blues songs.

Ukulele Song Books 1 and 2: Many folk and popular songs are written out with words and chords in these two books.

Musicophilia: Tales of Music and the Brain, Revised and Expanded Edition by Oliver Sacks: A scientific exploration of music's physical effect on the human brain. Full of interesting real world stories.

This is Your Brain on Music by Daniel Levitin: Explains our physical and emotional attachment to music, using hundreds of contemporary artists and songs as examples.